SYLVIA LAWSON

Sylvia Lawson writes cultural history, journalism and fiction. Her work includes the multi-award winning *The Archibald Paradox*, on the early Sydney *Bulletin* and its principal editor; collections of stories and essays, *How Simone de Beauvoir Died in Australia* and *Demanding the Impossible: seven essays on resistance*; *The Outside Story*, a novel centred on the Sydney Opera House. She is currently film critic for the online and print journal *Inside Story*.

In memory of Martin Williams (1948–2012)
and Paul Willemen (1944–2012)
filmworkers, film-thinkers, my friends

AUSTRALIAN SCREEN CLASSICS

the back of beyond

SYLVIA LAWSON

CURRENCY PRESS,
SYDNEY

NATIONAL
FILM
&SOUND
ARCHIVE

First published by Currency Press Pty Ltd and the NFSA in 2013.

Currency Press Pty Ltd
PO Box 2287, Strawberry Hills
NSW 2012 Australia
enquiries@currency.com.au
www.currency.com.au

National Film & Sound Archive
GPO Box 2002, Canberra
ACT 2601 Australia
www.nfsa.gov.au

Australian Screen Classics series: ISSN 1447-557X

National Library of Australia—Cataloguing-in-Publication Data:

Author:	Lawson, Sylvia.
Title:	The back of beyond / Sylvia Lawson.
ISBN:	9780868199757 (pbk.)
Series:	Australian screen classics
Notes:	Includes bibliographical references.
Subjects:	The Back of Beyond (Motion picture).
	Motion pictures, Australian.
	Feature films—Australia—History and criticism.

Dewey Number: 791.4372

Cover design by Katy Wall for Currency Press
Typeset by Katy Wall for Currency Press in Iowan Old Style roman 9.5 pt.
Printed by Fineline Print & Copy Service, St Peters, NSW.
All images within the text are reproduced with the kind permission of Crecy den Hollander and the Heyer family.

AUSTRALIAN
SCREEN CLASSICS

JANE MILLS
Series Editor

Our national cinema plays a vital role in our cultural heritage and in showing us at least something of what it is to be Australian. But the picture can get blurred by unruly forces such as competing artistic aims, inconstant personal tastes, political vagaries, constantly changing priorities in screen education and training, technological innovation and the market.

When these forces remain unconnected, the result can be an artistically impoverished cinema and audiences who are disinclined to seek out and derive pleasure from a diverse range of films, including Australian ones.

This series is a part of screen culture which is the glue needed to stick these forces together. It's the plankton in the moving image food chain that feeds the imagination of our filmmakers and their audiences. It's what makes sense of the opinions, memories, responses, knowledge and exchange of ideas about film.

Above all, screen culture is informed by a love of cinema. And it has to be carefully nurtured if we are to understand and appreciate the aesthetic, moral, intellectual and sentient value of our national cinema.

Australian Screen Classics will match some of our best-loved films with some of our most distinguished writers and thinkers, drawn from the worlds of culture, criticism and politics. All we ask of our writers is that they feel passionate about the films they choose. Through these thoughtful, elegantly-written books, we hope that screen culture will work its sticky magic and introduce more audiences to Australian cinema.

Jane Mills is Associate Professor & Deputy Director of the Journalism & Media Research Centre at the University of New South Wales.

CONTENTS

I

BEFORE TELEVISION, AFTER GRIERSON

It was a strange little film from the beginning; now as I write, it is almost sixty years old. Once upon a time, as a newspaper cadet—picking up a free ticket which nobody else in the office wanted—I sat in the Shell company's Sydney theatrette and watched, with complete astonishment, a story about an outback postman taking mail and supplies across the Central Australian desert: a production from the Shell Film Unit, but hardly a film you could describe as promotion for a brand of petrol.

Its visions of space and desert had a kind of radiance, and so I came out from that screening feeling a new kind of connection with Australia, or rather with a new idea of Australia, the country I was born in, and a country I didn't know. Though I'd taken in some lively documentaries in student film society screenings—a few things like Harry Watt's and Basil Wright's wonderful *Night Mail*, and *Fires Were Started*, Humphrey Jennings' great wartime poem on London under the blitz—I didn't expect anything really engaging from Australian documentary; I thought it was all mere information (how they make paper, how they built bridges, the life-cycle of the koala). The strangeness of the work I'd just seen had to do with an extraordinary orchestration of document with re-enactment, and with the storytelling offered by its characters. Through many viewings since, *The Back of Beyond* keeps its emotional charge, even while it changes with history and distance, seeming to connect differently each time with the moment in which I'm watching. I don't know how often I've seen it, through the decades of its life and mine; I've used it in both adult education and university classes, in courses with names like Film and Politics and Images of Australia.

I watch it again in January 2012 with an acutely critical companion, who first saw it as an immigrant schoolboy sometime in the early 1960s. Now he finds it astonishing, and wonders why anyone ever took its images, its version of things, for granted; and both of us stare into the film's date, 1954. We say: but this was the last minute before television! and the date matters; a few years later, *The Back of Beyond* would have been impossible—or at least, a very different project. The documentary tradition which shaped both its visible perspectives and its spoken language (the overriding, voice-of-God commentary) was coming to its end. The pre-television documentary genre matches visual with verbal poetry; takes care of pictorial values, considers composition in every shot, and looks at individuals and society with a careful, humane benevolence. When Eric Else wrote in 1968 that John Heyer's *The Back of Beyond* was probably 'the last of the great romantic documentaries' he was looking back across the technological and cultural divide to the British poetic documentary movement of the 1930s and '40s, and such films as *Coal Face*, *Night Mail*, *Listen to Britain*, *Fires Were Started*, and perhaps further back to the early work of the American pioneer Robert Flaherty in *Nanook of the North* and *Moana*.

That tradition, which was absorbed and taken seriously by John Heyer, has often been called Griersonian, in salute to the lasting influence of the founding father whose purposeful social ethic and instructional style had shaped British documentary from the early 1930s. John Grierson, running film units within government bureaucracies, practised a definite, teacherly philosophy: the documentary was to be promoted and pursued not for its own sake, but for democracy and social betterment, and especially for the sake of international dialogue and understanding. Grierson's sisters, Ruby and Marion Grierson, were also documentary film-makers, whose work should be better-known.[1] But founders and teachers are often left behind; in the most vividly enduring films from Grierson's group, ethics and aesthetics come together, and the instructional intent drops away. Like those, *The Back of Beyond* is a crafted essay, a highly planned exploration. From the outset, it was intensively *written*; Heyer's wife Janet, herself an artist, had a hand in the script; so did two eminent Australian poets, Douglas Stewart, then literary editor of the weekly *Bulletin*, and Roland Robinson.

While the film is centred on one person, there's no interest in psychology or biography; we take our truck driver as we find him, as he is. The Griersonian director doesn't probe. Nor does he (it was almost never she) trade in politics; the liberal values of civil society, with consensus round the twinned ideas of democracy and progress, are always to be assumed. My viewing companion observed that John Heyer was interestingly apolitical, that he was aiming for a broad human picture, and that in consequence the Aboriginal presence in the film's story was something calmly taken on: as the film sees Aboriginal people, they belong. They're not seen as involving 'social problems' (in the language of that day),

3

The director takes a tea break.

nor as desolate and marginal; they share the world of the Track, and most of the time they're sharing its work. In that particular respect, the film upsets our stereotypes of the 1950s. It offers a special field of vision, and within its framework it is not racist; that very fact is part of its eloquence over the long term, its potency for us in the twenty-first century.

II
'A CARRIER CALLED KRUSE'

Music, a sombre meditation for brass and strings, moves under the credits and the narration that follows. An introduction appears, in elegant typeface on a background of furrowed sand:

> The development of inland Australia largely depends on the men who keep open the supply-lines and communications— the outback mailmen. In an area larger than Europe, beyond the last roads and railways... their tracks make the map of the inland—become the roads of tomorrow—and mark the growth of the Nation. This is the story of one of them, and the people he serves—

Growth, development, Nation with a capital N; there is much in the film that will undercut those notions of progress. The map of the continent comes up, with a glow at the centre, a near-empty area unmarked by towns; a high aerial shot of the road through the desert—'a thousand miles from anywhere... a lane through the burning centre of Australia, the Birdsville track.' The narration lifts and expands over images that are highly composed, painterly; a bird swoops across a glowing, immaculate sky, and I think again in passing how it was that black and white film always seemed to register Australian skies more vividly than colour film has ever done. A frilled lizard, a small desert dragon, rears up on a rock. Cut back to the bird, back to the lizard; classic montage, constructed visual interplay with slow music, reiterating the non-human, the ancient and alien. The camera moves in across the sand to hold on a large, dark whorled shell, a spectacular fossil. About these shots there's a stark, surrealist hyper-reality; we could be looking at images by Salvador Dali.

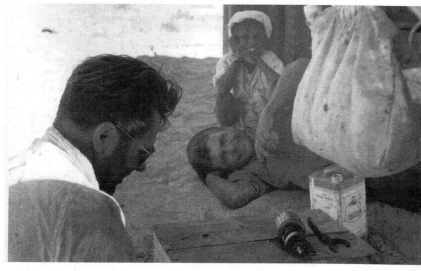

Resting in the shade of the truck, Tom Kruse, with Henry and Paddy.

The narrator remembers the old quest for the inland sea, and the arrival of the explorers Sturt and Eyre 'twelve million years too late.' There is an explorer's memory, a quote from Sturt's journal: as he crested a desert ridge, he believed that he would finally see a stretch of water 'with white-capped waves', but instead there was only the endless sand, the flat horizon, blankness disappearing 'into the mirage and off the edge of the world'. What he saw 'closed all my dreams', he wrote, and named the crest Mount Hopeless. Against the bare ground there are white animal skeletons and skulls; the narrator reflects on the remains of ancient life, the fish and shells and diprotodon bones 'mingled with those of the horse, the camel'—here the tone drops, grimly—'and the white man'. But then too there is the Aborigine, 'part of a vanishing race.'

All this is high lament; the poetry of loss surrounds the act of looking, evoking words from T.S. Eliot's *The Waste Land* ('Here is no water but only rock'). Then there is a decisive change of register; the intensity drops. A long trail of cattle moves across the sand. 'After the explorers came the settlers'; for each of them, the nearest neighbour could be a hundred miles away. It's 120 degrees Fahrenheit (49 degrees Celsius) in the shade, and 'the only shade is the shadow of the truck.' That truck, a solid Leyland Badger, comes heaving unevenly over a hill of sand. We move in on the cabin, to be introduced to 'a carrier called Kruse: Tom Kruse.' The words are given emphasis and resonance, as though introducing us to a heroic identity; but Tom will not be that. The driver's door carries the words 'E.G. Kruse/Marree'; the commentary doesn't tell us that his given names were Esmond Gerald.

William Henry Butler (left) and Tom Kruse loading the Leyland Badger mail-truck.

Bringing the rig to a stop and getting out, checking the tension on the ropes, he's revealed as someone amiably pragmatic, a stocky, unpretentious man with a friendly face. At the time of the filming, Kruse was just forty. One thing is clear immediately: he's a man at home with his job. He is on easy, matter-of-fact terms with the two Aborigines who share the ride, his offsider Henry—named in the credits as William Henry Butler—who shares the cabin, and Paddy. The latter is a cheerful small boy, who looks about eight; he's cuddled under a blanket on top of the high load, along for the ride. The truck gets bogged in sand; then Paddy's out there helping, plainly anxious to prove his value. He's seen at close quarters, vigorously digging up the sand around the tyre; then from a camera position on ground level under the tail of the truck, we see his face, concentrating on the job. These shots are about his energy, and also about his need to be part of the whole adventure.

Then, from a point somewhere above it, we see the truck circling on a flat stretch of earth to gather speed. Cut to close shots, the sand flying up round the churning tyres; they make it over the rise with the help of sheets of iron, some left by the roadside, some carried on the truck. These are replaced; Henry and Paddy are seen furiously chasing the truck as it moves downhill. That's almost the last we see of Paddy; he becomes a positive absence. 'Every fortnight the story begins' runs the narration, and we go back to where Tom Kruse's trip starts; we could be looking at more than one journey.

Marree began as a depot for Afghan cameleers in the 1870s, and developed with the building of the Overland Telegraph. Now in the time of the film, in this 'ragged flower of a town' in northeast

Heyer persuades the elderly Afghan guide, Bejah Dervish, to become a film actor.

South Australia—tin and 'corrugated iron, shimmering in the corrugated air'—modern Australian multiculturalism is foreshadowed; the commentary observes 'black men, white men, Afghans' (eliding the female presences, visible though they are). Tom is greeted by Bejah, 'the giant Afghan'; he's old, tall, turban'd, immensely dignified. Once, we're told, he led a trail of fifty camels out here, and 'fought the desert by compass and by Koran'. He is seen taking his prayer-mat to a stony ridge: 'Allah is great, Allah is great...' He speaks a prayer for his kinsman Abdul, who died out here in the hot wilderness 'far from the mountains of his homeland'; a woman is seen, moving among graves, scattering water and wheat grains while the prayer goes on. Bejah kneels and bows repeatedly—'Allah is great...'; the voice dies away, he gathers the mat and himself, and is last seen from above, a lone figure moving away on the hard earth. It is one of the sequences which, looked at all these decades later, deepen the film and open its boundaries; Bejah's presence is not to be summarised, not to be tied off into a containable pattern.

The big train is seen arriving at the station—'steaming up from Adelaide, six hundred miles into Australia'… Here, Heyer was inflating the facts; the distance from Adelaide to Marree is only 426 miles (686 kilometres). But he practised a thematics of distance; almost every shot in the film is in some way about great spaces, while the mileages recur through the narration. The train's arrival makes a beautifully classic shot, calling up pleasures from the dawn of cinema and early Westerns. The young John Heyer spent hours in film society screenings, where he learnt his history of the cinema; he must have watched the Lumières' views of workers leaving the factory, parents feeding their baby in the garden, and the arrival of the train at the station at La Ciotat.[2] The shot in *The Back of Beyond* repeats, precisely, the dynamic angle those first documentarists took on the puffing engine in 1895, with the people waiting on the platform.

Sacks and boxes are moved from train to truck. While they work, Henry wants some music; he opens a portable gramophone and puts on a record, light piano blues. Tom notices a package marked 'fragile'. 'Fragile' he says. 'Here—put it in behind the spuds.' We see the offhand bushman; we also see that he will take due care. To get beyond Marree northeast into the desert, there's only the truck—but there's room to wonder about other means of transport, as a cart pulled by two camels, driven by white men, moves toward the station. In the back two Aboriginal women appear—big women, mothers or grandmothers, in headscarves, floral cotton and cardigans, one holding a toddler. Elsewhere in the town, a youngish white woman is found helping an older black one write a family letter, with news of comings and goings. 'What else you want to tell 'em, Mary?' 'Love (from) Mary'; the letter must be ready for Tom to carry. It's a momentary detail, and we might take it for granted: white woman being kind to black one, who is illiterate; this was normality. Now if not then, a further thought could be spared: such instances of benign tutelage were no doubt scattered across the outback. In the world of the town this black woman seems like a dependant, someone at a complete disadvantage; but what don't we know about her? Those we saw riding in the camel cart are like her, dependant on the white man's transport; but they are also responsible for children. We don't hear the language or languages in which they are at home; we don't see their own authority.

As Tom and Henry heave and stack the mailbags, Tom's wife Valma (but her name is not heard) emerges from a doorway to tell him his dinner's getting cold, and ask him how far he's likely to get by tonight; he thinks he'll manage 60 miles (100 kilometres), as far as Dulkaninna.[3] At this point, if not earlier, the strain in the spoken dialogue is particularly apparent. In the process of re-recording, the film's talk has been re-enacted, and somewhat overacted in the process; while the wording itself is natural and probable enough, the delivery is often hard to credit. One story is that the sound tapes were damaged by the hot conditions of filming, making the re-enactments necessary; in any event, Heyer re-recorded all the dialogue—some of it with actors, some with the original speakers.

But with the glimpse of Valma, the performed speech provokes a question of whether the director did not flatten her into an entirely predictable part. There might imaginably have been a sight of the house Tom lives in, of a life between the mail-runs; but that was never what Heyer set himself to look at. Out of his very ordinariness, this 'carrier called Kruse' centres the observer's attention, though he gives no sign of wanting it. Tom Kruse isn't interested in himself; his interest is in negotiating the Track as it is on the day, on getting the job done. He doesn't want the letters that arrive for him in Marree as he's about to set off; it's a little ironic that while he carries mail for others, postage for himself is received as a nuisance, something threatening to hold him up on his journey. As it later transpires, one letter is from a salesman urging 'hauling for profit'; on the other, handwritten and evidently more personal, we get no information. The thrust of the sequence is the loading of the truck, with Tom calling the destinations: Dulkaninna, Etadinna, Mulka, Mungerannie, Clifton Hills, Pandie Pandie, Birdsville.* On each journey there are choices to be made, since in fact there are three tracks, middle, inner and outer. 'Which way you going?' asks Henry. 'Over the sandhills, or across the creek?' 'Over the top!' says Tom emphatically, in the tone of a driver glad to be hitting the road.

Some commentators have called Tom a nomad; the term is rather too romantic. He's above all a bushman, with work to do, intrepidly good-humoured and resourceful. He grew up as one of twelve children in a struggling farming family in outback South Australia; he worked for a blacksmith, then as a garage hand before

The mail truck stops at Dulkaninna, a homestead no longer shown on the maps.

* The spellings of place-names are variable. Marree appears sometimes as Maree, Mungerannie as Mungeranie, Etadinna as Etadunna.

starting the cross-country mail service from the little town of Yunta, and learning the tracks between there and Birdsville. His way with a bogged-down truck is typical—'we'll have her going in two ups'. He says little, so the sentences are vivid: 'You never know what the old Cooper's going to do' (meaning Cooper Creek); 'All OK, Mrs Mac, all OK'; 'This won't buy the baby a new dress'. As the truck trundles into Birdsville, our last sight of Tom is of the matter-of-fact driver, breaking into smiles, finishing his job for the moment. We like him, and the little we know of him is all we need to know for the film's purposes.

III
ON TO THE TRACK

A sign tells us that it's 325 miles to Birdsville—523 kilometres in today's measurement. From Marree, the laden rig moves away toward empty distance; then the angle is reversed, and it's bumping along towards us. Two small white boys come running in from screen left, calling to Tom to let them ride as far as the gate; he stops, and they clamber on to the load. Their entry has a set-piece look to it, something too obviously directed; but we can believe in the fun the kids had swinging on the gate, opening and shutting it for Tom (didn't all country town kids do this at track and railway crossings?) and can believe that in Marree, this was a fortnightly treat. The images would not have looked stilted for outback people in 1954; they weren't used to seeing themselves and their places on the screen.

Skies, birds, wilderness occupy the fields of vision; the film lifts away into other spaces. The story remembers its seasons; those when the cattle died of thirst—their corpses are unburied on the sand; and then in the floods, when the skulls of drowned beasts hang in the trees. Along the way the mail truck crosses bare, stony expanses; this is not that Central Australian territory where the tough little shrubs and flowers, oak and mulga make

With Heyer and other crew members, Ross Wood takes an angle from the ground on the mail truck..

the ground into beautiful desert parkland. It's one hot, iron gibber plain, broken only by the artesian bore, with the hot water steaming and bubbling up. The narration here is dark poetry: 'All tastes like dust in the mouth/ All strikes like iron in the mind.'

It's looking now, not then, that I'm arrested by those lines; the mouth and mind called up are not those of Tom Kruse or his kind. They belong with the stories of the nineteenth century explorers driven crazy by heat and emptiness; they set Tom Kruse's job, his way of handling it and belonging to this desert track, against the trackless desolations that surrounded Leichhardt, Sturt, Burke and Wills. Behind him and the people in places like Marree, Mulka and Birdsville there are those unforgiving histories, and the unanswerable questions which the film raises more than once through its course: why go there? Why try to live there?

Then they're driving into the night; for a moment which must have been awkward for Tom, with the camera on the bonnet, we look at him through the windscreen, and see his determination to keep going on schedule. Stark, ghostly branches catch the headlights. When they stop to clear an obstacle, Henry remembers fixing a broken-down vehicle with gears improvised from coolibah wood—'good wood, coolibah'; Tom laughs at him, and Henry has to admit that the wooden gears didn't last long. The creatures appear to watch them, here an owl, there a dingo, and there, sliding over the sand, a long and particularly beautiful snake; but men and beasts are never in frame together. The danger is part of the desert world; it's there, it can wait.

They reach Etadinna and the Oldfields, who run a vast property 'with a few native stockmen'. The first shot in the sequence shows one of those stockmen packing up a swag. Meanwhile Mrs Ida Oldfield is operating the radio from a desk on the closed verandah, swapping news with her neighbour Dora in Mulka up the Track. It's clear that the radio sustains a crucial news and gossip circuit; a child has the measles, there's a dust storm coming, and Tom is arriving; time to boil the kettle. Tom joins Mr Jim Oldfield, and reports that around the area 'dingoes are the biggest problem'. Henry unloads the gramophone, the 'music machine'; he says 'the kids'll be waiting'. Aboriginal children come running across the sand; there's a glimpse of a humpy, a very poor dwelling, but it's incidental to the brief sequence where Henry sits with them in a circle; there's one white child among them, and they're all clapping to a barn-dance tune. This time, there's more spontaneity in the filming. 'Happy darkies?' asks a present-day viewer drily: but other views are possible. Out there in the endless sands, those kids knew how to have some fun.

The men sit down together; Ida brings the tea, and Jim does the talking. We hear of an Aboriginal worker, Malcolm, who is regrettably leaving the property, and realise that we've already seen him packing up. 'Wants to get back to his own country. Good stockman, too', Mr Oldfield remarks philosophically, but, he says, you can't keep them—meaning Aborigines—when they decide to go. Henry is not seen at the tea table; he's out there with the

Heyer directs the cinematographer Ross Wood as Tom Kruse rolls a petrol drum.

Tom Kruse, Malcolm Arkaringa and Henry camped by the Cooper, Tom at the radio.

kids. Back at the radio, Ida tells them at Mulka (43.5 kilometres, or 27 miles up the track) that 'Tom should get to the Cooper by tonight and do the crossing tomorrow.'

Cooper Creek is a legendary watercourse of alternating character—now a spread of dry gullies, then a network of shallow streams, and now, in the time of the film, a vast moving lake. Tom and Henry leave the truck on the shore, and transfer all of its load by barge to the other side, where a second truck is parked. The transfer takes a day, six or seven loads. Now Tom has two helpers, both Henry and Malcolm Arkaringa. The laden barge rocks on the water; adjusting ropes and loads, checking balance, Tom falls in; he swims about, and some viewers find it odd that Malcolm does not reach out a hand to help him. Was there an unspoken convention that black and white didn't touch? No; Malcolm is simply busy with the engine. In close shot, he turns: 'Where *is* that feller Kruse?'

This sequence is about sharing, camaraderie, lightness, the living-out of roles. They camp beside the Cooper; Henry cooks the meat. All kinds of freight are unloaded, including a substantial armchair and a headless dressmaker's model—a slim, curvy abstract of the female body. The light jazz on the soundtrack goes back to piano blues as Tom begins to dance, while the other two laugh at him; then he grasps the model by the waist, waltzes around with it, sets it down, takes off his hat and bows. In this, one of the film's best-remembered sequences, the comedy has a disconcerting, surreal kind of edge; we're suddenly asked to remember that in this desert place men must work and travel for long periods without women. In a conversation in London in 1991, John Heyer told me that his wife Janet, who died in 1969, had objected to the sequence; as one of his co-writers, she thought it should be cut. He didn't go into her reasons. Perhaps she thought that this film of a journey, a men's enterprise, had no need to take sex into account, even as comedy.

After the dance, human distress breaks in; Tom's radio catches a call for help for the flying doctor, who obviously isn't receiving it; a woman alone on her property is suffering increasing pain and loss of vision. Even if the dubbed-in voices somewhat undermine belief, it's still credible evidence of an outback crisis.

Henry and Malcolm pause over their meal; they look alert and anxious. Tom—steadily matter-of-fact, brushing away the flies as he speaks—relays the message to the doctor, who promises to reach her. The fragment of narrative tails away; we never know just what happens to 'Mrs Mac'.[4]

Shadowed by the broken-down buildings of an old mission, they make camp near Jack the Dogger, a lone hunter who traps dingoes and collects hides and scalps at one pound a time. Jack wields a formidable knife; he's a misanthrope, hardbitten and gloomy, wanting to get out of the place. Tom tells him he's been out here on his own too long, while Malcolm moves off alone among the ruins. This place was once

John Heyer standing at the back of a vehicle with radio equipment.

called Kopperamanna, and here once a Lutheran missionary, Father Vogelsang, gathered 500 Aborigines around him in community. Malcolm remembers, in voice-over; we don't see him speaking, but register the sadness in his face, artfully lit against the night. This, he says, was good country; he was born here, and Father Vogelsang 'grew him up'. They had their store, church and school; 'this was our promised land', and this was the place for which Malcolm needed to leave Etadinna. There is the sound of the vanished congregation singing in liturgy; the camera moves over the crumbling stone walls, the worn timbers of old, rough-hewn pews; the surmounting cross, the skeleton of a water-cart, and the iron frame of what was once a lectern. The image is stark, black, skeletal. Malcolm stands at Father Vogelsang's grave, a formal tombstone inside an iron fence. (There's a question here; Malcolm seems quite young, somewhere in his thirties; but we see from the date on the tombstone that Father Vogelsang died in 1913.)

Thus the film grasps briefly at another story, the Lutherans' evangelism in Central Australia, and the early Christianising of the Aborigines. Long before historians began taking up the work and life of that earlier missionary, Carl Strehlow, viewers of *The Back of Beyond* learned a little about Father Herrman Heinrich Vogelsang, who, in Malcolm's lament, travelled across the desert for 'thirty days and thirty nights' to the place where he established the mission.[5] There are stark material ghosts: the iron skeletons of the lectern and the water-cart. But the central figure here is Malcolm, wandering the remains of a colonial project; would anyone in the 1950s audiences have asked why he mourns the mission, and not his own people's tribal life and country? We seem to be invited toward an elegy, both for lost Aboriginal life and for the white man's ambitions as well. There was little consciousness then of

21

the extent of dispossession; and in an Australia dominated by rapidly expanding suburbs in its coastal cities, there was little sense either of those white histories which had vanished in the short 170 years of European settlement. The ruins of the Lutheran mission still give shelter to travellers, but for viewers then and later, they are signs of the coloniser's defeat.

The elegiac mode gives place to the everyday, to the weathered good humour of Tom in the battered, jolting truck, laden as it is with sacks, packages, drums of water and fuel. As the story continues, the vehicle looks more and more like a bizarre Heath Robinson assemblage, with low angles on the front tyres, splayed

Heyer directing his principal cast, with a fully-laden Ford Blitz truck.

as the rig bumps along toward the camera. As for the 'vanishing race': we've met Paddy, Mary and her cohort; and Tom's driving mate is the practical Henry, who knows about coolibah wood, about driving over sandhills, cooking and managing a raft. Thus the film's account of Aboriginality divides; the people Paddy belongs to don't look like vanishing any time soon. They share the desert with Bejah, unrolling his prayer mat on the sands; with Jack and Joe the Rainmaker, and the unnamed white woman who helps the black one write her letter for delivery by Tom Kruse.

The truck crosses another hot, flat plain. The commentary surveys 'a sea of sand and stone; who passes or perishes, only the dingo knows'. For a moment again, the mournful verbal poetry overrides the visual, and we can almost hear the dingo howling into the wind, the animal taking over human grief. Tom reaches Mulka, 'the loneliest store on earth'; we get only a passing glimpse of those who live there. Here the narrator says that we're halfway to Birdsville; on the map, however, it looks as though there are still two-thirds of the Track to go; and the filmed journey moves rather quickly over the next 75 miles (121 kilometres). The truck crests another sandhill, and reaches Clifton Hills, the last of the five stations along the Track—five, where once there were fifteen:

> The others have gone, beaten by loneliness and drought, and their homes reduced to a windswept grave, a crumbling wall. Proud homes, built foursquare and hard, broken by the relentless cycle of the sun, until all that remains is the music of their names: Mirra Mitta, Appatunkna, Killalpapina, Oorawillani... [voice fading] Oorawillani... their stories live on in the tales and legends of the Track...

The narration is a bridge to one of the film's best remembered and most troubling episodes, the story of the two lost children.

'It was early September, so the story goes...' A woman's voice comes over on the radio, with rising anxiety: 'Hello Jessie—are you there, Jessie—are you there, Jessie?' The camera moves through a house with signs of housework half-done, an uncleared meal table, and finds the body of a woman fallen on the ground; this mother has suddenly died. The narrator tells us that the elder of the two sisters, Sally (who looks about ten), did not understand the radio, and decided that they should make their way to the Track to find help. We see two little girls, in dresses, sunhats, shoes and socks, with dog and billy-cart, setting out across the sand; cresting hills, crossing their own tracks, the younger one, Roberta, piping on a toy flute. With their water running low, they tie the dog to a tree; cut from the engaging black spaniel to an advancing snake. The children vanish; two days later their father follows their tracks, unavailingly: 'Into the ocean of sand they went; no one knows what became of them. All that remains is their story.'

Viewers have said they find this part of the film heart-rending, even while conscious of its manifest fiction. The narrator has signalled towards 'the stories and legends of the Track', so that the re-enactment does not seem forced or false; it's helped by the children, pretty good actors both, who were recruited in Marree. One detail is clearly authentic, the weatherworn timber gravepost with Jessie's name. The tale, however, is one that viewers mull over compulsively: was it possible that a ten-year-old, growing up in that setting, couldn't have learned to handle the radio, or known her way to the Track? Stories of lost children haunt Australian history and folklore, and the desert is harsher than the bush. On the film's emotional path, the way it works in memory, the sandstorm which overtakes Tom in the following sequence blows backward over the children. He and Henry, camped under trees, wake to wild wind and dust; they scramble to get their boots on and run for the truck.

Further along the Track, they stop for a mother and daughter who stand waiting, dressed in their Sunday best; they're going to go shopping in Birdsville. The mother bends to tie the little girl's sunbonnet; it's a tiny moment of action, a shot freighted with meaning about due care

The lost children: two little girls, with dog and billy-cart, disappearing into the sand hills.

for children, a sense of quiet, symbolic restoration. Tom, a bush gentleman, lifts his hat as the two climb into the cabin; Henry sits in the armchair on top of the load; again, the image is both comic and surreal. The narration rises over the landscape, to contemplate the wayward lives of travellers in places like this, where a man can disappear if he needs to, going off to die in the desert, or else 'turn up on the coast with another name'—and 'where the police officer can write in his diary: Thomas Crow seems to be out of his mind. Sub-Inspector King shot himself on the station verandah. Another hot day.'

The line is at once pragmatic and shocking; this, with the sandstorms, the lost children, the abandoned homesteads, tells us again that the desert can win. Wherever the white men may have gone, Old Joe the Rainmaker goes on stamping on the stony ground, calling on the skies, beating the dust with his spray of hawk feathers, chanting: 'I am Nangarli, I bring the rain.' The narrator adds a line of Douglas Stewart's: 'And no rain falls/ Across the country.'

Then we're looking at the Birdsville Hotel, an impressive specimen of outback building; this is one of many remote settlements which hoped to be more than they are. Birdsville—in the time of the film, and still today—is the hotel, a large sports oval, and a scattering of iron-roofed houses under the relentless sun. A high, wide shot shows the truck in the middle distance; the community nurse, immaculate in white uniform and veil, turns from her gate to the radio, winds up the transmitter and picks up the microphone: 'Tom is arriving, Tom is arriving.' Radio voices come in from down the Track: 'Tom is arriving in Birdsville.' Elsewhere, an Aboriginal woman sits with children, black and white, in a circle; making shapes with her hands on the ground

between them, she is teaching 'the ancient lore of the sand', imparting the kind of knowledge that can save lives and sustain them. The children play around her; one of them looks like Paddy.

The reassuring jazz theme returns, lifting and speeding up. The truck comes rocking in; at the

'Old Joe the rain-maker... calls on the hawk-men to bring down the rain'.

wheel Tom is smiling broadly, visibly very happy; once more, they've made it. An old man, leaning on a stick, crosses Birdsville's main street to the post-office, a windowless, galvanised iron shed; he has the key for the padlock. Next door another man is also unlocking, opening up the bar. A few more people crowd in; the film ends with high-angle images of a small, peaceful outback community collecting its fortnightly mail, and three men heading for the bar.

IV
THE EDUCATION OF A DIRECTOR

Decades on from that first viewing, screening *The Back of Beyond* with students, I faced a startling mix of responses. Some loved it, while others thought it was truly awful; heavy-handed, inflated like a sermon, out of date. The sense of elocutionary strain in the re-enactments doesn't help. At those points the students laughed at the film's awkwardness; and when the solitary snake winds across the moonlit sand they said hey, that one was let out of somebody's hessian bag for sure. They laughed quite differently at the surreal comedy in the camp, when Tom dances with the headless model. I had to do some talking then about pre-televisual styles in documentary, about the inheritance from Grierson, about the love of intensely calculated 'composition' in images and highflown spoken commentary—always in ABC/BBC male voices. In all that I had to learn something more myself about what it means to be watching film historically. It means not only watching in the knowledge that the lives we meet along the Birdsville track are being lived in the early 1950s, but also that the film-maker's ways of seeing belong in that time as well.

At the 1954 Venice film festival, *The Back of Beyond* won the *Grand Prix Assoluto*, the award for the best film across all categories; it was praised for 'the perfect blending of words, sounds and images'. In the same year, as a documentary offered not as a support but as a feature, it was part of the first Sydney Film Festival, joining Rossellini's *Germany Year Zero*, Jacques Tati's *Jour de Fête* and René Clair's *Sous les Toits de Paris:* all revelations, all extending consciousness of the range and possibilities of cinema. David Donaldson, the festival's founding director, remembers that

> [w]e knew that he [Heyer] had been away a lot making it, indeed had given up chairing the festival committee. We had little idea what the film might be, certainly no thought of what it would become in release. Heyer kept being not quite ready with a print, week after week. I understand that at Supreme Sound he made 33, or perhaps it was 36, trial prints to get the best settings. The final, and marvellous, result came to hand with only days to spare.

There were more prizes, diplomas at festivals in Edinburgh, Capetown, Johannesburg and Trento, and a first prize at Montevideo in 1956. In Australia it was seen by some 750,000 people in its first two years, and by schoolchildren everywhere for at least a decade after that. The film scholar Brian Shoesmith—who also was an English immigrant then—remembers how he had not been in Australia very long as a child when

> suddenly the school was closed down so we could all trot off to the local shire hall in Bunbury [WA] to see The Back of Beyond. … So it was circulated as an exemplary text for children to see to understand something of this nation. It was a very strange experience for a 13 or 14 year old English kid to be suddenly pulled out of school to partake of this national ritual.

On its first appearances, large claims were made; it was praised for unforced humour, for balancing poetry, imagination and realism. The philosopher Alan Stout, one of the most energetic proponents of Australian film, called it 'a landmark in Australian documentary' and the *Manchester Guardian* went further: '... one of the most remarkable documentaries ever made.' An unnamed reviewer in the BBC's weekly *The Listener* wrote that documentary 'has rarely been less self-conscious or more enthralling.' 'Once more' wrote Dilys Powell in the London *Sunday Times* 'the Shell film-makers revive faith in documentary'. She also wrote that the film showed 'a landscape where man is always solitary, always on the defensive against Nature.' *The Sydney Morning Herald*'s anonymous reviewer wrote that the film

> is bound to rank as an Australian masterpiece [while] the message... is by no means one of unrelieved horror and pessimism. There is much hopefulness in the unaffected courage and the humour it finds among the people who live along the Birdsville Track.

That local comment might have been intended as reassurance for suburban audiences who might find the desert story confronting. Watching and reading now, the most interesting of those early comments is *The Listener*'s:

> The final effect is a wholly convincing search for truth and much skill in presenting it... A vividly fascinating film which sheds a forbidding light on Australian realities and darkens one's suspicions of the universe...

So *The Back of Beyond* established itself as a film always to be taken as a key moment in Australian film history in general, not only in the special register of documentary. It also remains alive in those spaces where film is understood as bearing on wider histories, as a story and a group of images that count in national self-understanding; and so it became a film that people love and remember. Much of what's being delivered is—after all—an array of reassuringly ordinary, knowable human figures; and yet we're still looking at the foreign country of the desert in mid-century, and at moments it seems immeasurably distant.

In the documentary canon, it retains its status, and it's because of this film that John Heyer has been called 'the father of Australian documentary'. He was born in Devonport, Tasmania, in 1916, to a certain level of privilege; his father was a doctor, and he was educated at Scotch College, one of Melbourne's high-ranking private schools for boys. He seems to have been a cinephile from the outset; while serving an apprenticeship to a firm of scientific instrument-makers, he went to night school to learn film projection and sound-recording. At 18, he worked briefly for Efftee Films, Frank Thring's company, which went out of business in 1935; Heyer then joined Cinesound Productions, and in the following two years worked as a camera assistant and assistant sound recordist on three features, Charles Chauvel's ambitious but unsuccessful epic *Heritage,* Ken Hall's *Thoroughbred,* and Edward G. Bowen's *White Death.* In 1940 he was one of the four-member camera team for exteriors on Chauvel's best and biggest enterprise, *Forty Thousand Horsemen,* with Frank Hurley, Bert Nicholas and Tasman Higgins (the principal cinematographer was George Heath). In 1942, he married Dorothy Greenhalgh, who was always known as Janet; they had two daughters and a son.

Then in 1944, Harry Watt made him second-unit director on *The Overlanders,* and the experience was decisive. Heyer went with his cameraman 2500 kilometres along the Murranji track, from Western Australia across the Northern Territory and into Queensland; with the footage from that journey, he said, Harry

Watt 'was able to exploit one of the most cinematic of themes—
Man against Nature', and so

> gave himself a sweep of the country that ranged from open
> grass plains to rugged valleys and that typified by its hard,
> bright light and endless horizon, by its slender ghost-gums
> and eroded hills, the shapes and forms that are the essential
> Australia.

Thus in his early career Heyer worked with the small, beleaguered
Australian industry's most esteemed professionals; and film was
his intellectual world as well. With his close friend, the great
cinematographer Damien Parer, he read film criticism and theory
in such journals as the American *Experimental Cinema* and the
English *Close-Up*, *Monthly Film Bulletin* and the rigorous, wide-
ranging *Penguin Film Review*. He was active in the then-thriving film
society movement; he was president of the Sydney Film Society
and also of the Australian Council of Film Societies, and he argued
strongly for government involvement in national film production.

In those circles Eisenstein's theory and practice were essential
film knowledge; all serious cinephiles of the day knew the force
of the Kuleshov montage experiment, whereby the same shot
of a man's face is juxtaposed alternately with other images—a
plate of soup, a dead child, a desirable woman—setting up
vivid associations, so that the viewer seems to see the man's
expression changing after each one. Film society programmes
regularly included Eisenstein's *Battleship Potemkin*, *Strike* and
Ivan the Terrible, the essential early classics of montage; but they
also took in the lyrical documentary-essay work of the American
pioneer Robert Flaherty in *Nanook of the North* and *Louisiana Story*,
with their flowing style and long takes, and Pare Lorentz' poetic
and powerful essay *The River*.

Thus the cinephiles of Heyer's and Parer's generation were exposed to major contrasts in cinema styles and philosophies. They saw the classic British documentaries, including Grierson's own film *Drifters*—the only film for which he was credited as director, though he also directed an eleven-minute short, *Granton Trawler*. *Drifters* set the tradition which has been named Griersonian. It was centred on the drama of the herring fleet, the trawler setting out into rough weather, but little was seen of the turbulent seas; all the concentration was on the work below decks with pistons and winches, the two miles of nets paying out, and the catch, the salting, the delivery to worldwide transport. As in Wright's and Watt's *Night Mail,* and in the work of Cavalcanti, Jennings and others of the group, the stress was on process, labour, people as workers.

V

TRACKING DOCUMENTARY

From that distant film-cultural world, two emphases emerge decisively: one, that certain documentary films were unquestionably parts of the wider cinema canon. Two, that documentary was quite definitely marked off from drama and fiction, 'features'—even though most of the canonical documentaries, from the work of Robert Flaherty on, deploy elements of fiction and drama for their purposes. At the same time, there was no sense that documentary should be ranked below the feature-film as a lesser form. In later periods, documentary has often had to be argued for and defended against the view that it is no more than instructional, bare of performance, drama and narrative. But then, in the postwar, pre-television years and in a relatively favourable political climate, it stood in its own light, not simply as a group of film works, but a whole definable movement, even a cause to be defended.

In 1940 John Grierson went travelling in the British dominions to survey the situation for national production institutions, report to governments and make recommendations. His reports were made in the light of wartime information needs, but they were also far-sighted; the idea of a national film board in each of the dominions meant, in Grierson's view, a way of establishing international discussion, meeting across cultural boundaries. In Canada especially, his recommendations gave rise to action when the Canadian National Film Board was established, to global benefit; Canada's lively, inventive documentaries were seen everywhere. The Australian response was slow; unlike its British and Canadian equivalents, the Australian National Film Board (ANFB) was not set up early in wartime, nor was its establishment directly linked to Grierson's active promotion of a national documentary-producing institution. After his visit to Australia in 1940, Grierson's Memorandum to the Australian prime minister met with indifference—some have said outright hostility—from Robert Menzies.

That Memorandum[6] was a substantial document on the relations of government and film; Grierson thought the support of documentary far more important than any steps Australia might take toward commercial feature production. His main theme was the value of documentary in breaking down what he termed 'sectionalism' to 'induce a national viewpoint, by bringing alive Australia to itself in terms of films describing national effort', bringing 'the problems, responsibilities and achievements of Government' into 'the public imagination', and projecting 'a view of Australia as a powerful and progressive people'. Grierson proposed the appointment of an active national film committee led by qualified executives; in the short term, his proposals got no further than an inactive Cabinet sub-committee. This was during Menzies' brief tenure in early wartime, and was probably the reason for Grierson's generally sour view of Australia thereafter; later he told Stanley Hawes, then head of the Commonwealth Film Unit, that 'I have never been one to believe that God intended his sunshine to extend so promiscuously over the universe as to include Australia.'

At the end of the war, however, his proposals were taken up by the national Labor governments, successively of John Curtin and J.B. Chifley. When the National Film Board was established, John Heyer was appointed as producer-in-chief. In that role, he was part of the postwar Department of Information's (DOI) Film Division, the antecedent of the Commonwealth Film Unit and Film Australia. Most of its work was promotional, and in the larger projects this reached into advocacy. The intention was for a government-accredited body on the widely admired Canadian model; the DOI Film Division did not attain that level of prestige. Through successive stages, and working under difficulties, it did become the government's accredited producer of instructional documentary, generating—some would say—hundreds of hours of boredom for several generations of schoolchildren; many of those films are history now, in the most negative sense. But there was another side to it; for young people who wanted to work with film, the DOI Film Division was also a school of production training, almost the only one in that Australian period. Its limits had to be accepted; this was film in a specific national framework: worthy, solidly educational and progressive, according to particular ideas of progress.

Thus, through the years of John Heyer's development as a film worker and a director, Australian documentary was born and grew—not really into a flourishing adulthood, rather into a discontented early middle age.[7] Stanley Hawes came from England to lead the government film unit at its beginning; a young man then, with a promising reputation from his work with Grierson and Ralph Foster in Canada. Not long after arriving he made one particular documentary—the only one he directed—which at once expressed the ruling humanism of postwar aspirations and also, as it seems in long retrospect, set directions for a liberal-conservative future. This was *School in the Mailbox* (1946), which in a modest eighteen minutes, for the benefit of the inaugural conference of UNESCO in Paris, offered an account of the Australian correspondence school system.

Then, in the years between *School in the Mailbox* and *The Back of Beyond*, there was a change in the climate for documentary production. In December 1949, Labor lost government to the conservative coalition of Robert Menzies' Liberal Party with the Country Party, later the National Party. The Departments of Information and Post-war Reconstruction disappeared, and the DOI Film Division became part of the rather mysteriously-named Department of the Interior, thus keeping at least its initials. Its continued existence looked precarious; there were staff cuts, and more significantly, increased pressure to liberal-conservative conformity in the content and direction of its films. Through the following years, the young Turks of the Commonwealth Film Unit (CFU), as the DOI Film Division became, had perennial fun deriding and resisting the long regime of Hawes as producer-in-chief. 'I tried to preserve the Grierson philosophy and to continue the Grierson spirit' he said after his retirement. It was sometimes argued that his grey, cautious decency helped to keep the whole operation afloat, while more colourful practices might have imperilled it—though John Heyer, among others, thought that was nonsense. Whether or not Hawes sustained Grierson's active internationalism remains a question for the historians of the DOI/CFU; but John Heyer remained quite certain that *The Back of Beyond* could not have been made for the government.

But even with the limitations of the DOI, Heyer had his leading role. He could understand himself as part of a world-wide profession, and that was part of his apparent confidence—though he claimed to have been quite unconfident. He didn't have to feel embattled in the way which has marked the course of so many Australian film careers through the time between that day and this. During the early postwar years he made a series of instructional one-reelers; one of those, *Journey of a Nation* (1947) typifies the idealism of the period, a somewhat bombastic little essay on the need to unify Australia's absurdly differing railway gauges.

His most important commission for the ANFB issued in a remarkable thirty-six-minute essay on the Murray River and the communities along its 3,000-kilometre length, from the Snowy Mountains to Goolwa on the South Australian coast. This film, *The Valley is Ours* (1948), can be seen as one highly eloquent expression of the programme known as Post-war Reconstruction.[8] Between 1945 and Menzies' return to power in December 1949, that term named both a federal government department and a set of national projects: soldier settlement and immigration; large-scale primary production enabled by irrigation; concerted action against land erosion, drought, bushfire and the destruction of the forests; and regional development, breaking down the dominance of southeastern Australia's seaboard cities. Nationalism is signalled in the DOI's standard opening; a shot of the Australian flag flowing in the wind, martial music, and the title 'Australia Presents'. The narrator, Nigel Lovell, tells us: 'There is snow on the roof of Australia... the people of the valley wait for the thaw'. Spring is announced; clear drops fall into water. From there the film is a building symphony, with optimism rising from its elements: nature, forests, rolling hills and river, and the people living in apparently harmonious community, drawn together by forms of work linked to this geography. Watching more than sixty years later, we are sobered, knowing the Murray mightn't be flowing so strongly in our children's and grandchildren's futures. If audiences of the late 1940s could feel pride of place swelling up as they watched such a film, those of today might remember parents and grandparents, with a wry tolerance for lost illusions.

In *The Valley is Ours*, there are clear, recurring echoes of Lorentz' *The River*, made ten years earlier, and well-known by then to film society audiences. In both films, the narrator repeats the great distances covered, 4,023 kilometres for the Mississippi, 2,575 for the Murray; the litanies of names, the towns along the river, the smaller rivers that flow in to the larger one. Lorentz' film is made lyrical with Virgil Thomson's orchestral score; Sydney John Kay's music carries the flow in *The Valley is Ours*. Both films take up the penalties of intensive settlement, with de-afforestation, erosion, towns destroyed by flooding. In the American story, Lorentz looks at the poverty of share-croppers, with unforgettable images of cotton-pickers trailing their sacks, bodies bowed, toiling along the furrows. Heyer's observation is never quite so dark: children skipping and filing into school, the farming couple whose crop just escapes a destructive thunderstorm, men packed together shouting at the saleyards. What the two films have in common is more than subject-matter; it's a style, a way of registering a national project.

Perhaps Lorentz provided Heyer with a model; but both carried the signs of their antecedents. In ways which were decisive for their practice, Lorentz and Heyer were beneficiaries of that group which had formed around Grierson in the 1930s. For many students of cinema, *Drifters*, *Night Mail* and *Song of Ceylon* have become canonical names in a textbook list rather than living cinema, circulated and seen; and the British documentary movement sometimes looks dusty, virtuous, part of a leftish film culture which seems naïve and long out of date. But when those films are seen again, their vitality is startling; the dust is blown off, and while the commitment to fact and record is clear, so is the way those pre-war and wartime film makers grasped their moments and made the stories dance. *Night Mail* remains the ultimate film-poem, a symphony of rhythmic balances: the train's thunder and rattling, distance and closeness, verse and prose.

After *The Valley is Ours*, Heyer moved to the Shell Film Unit, rightly believing that it would give him greater freedom and scope, and took up the commission to make a film that would 'seek out the essence of Australianism and capture in celluloid the image and sound of the fundamental Australia.' At first sight, however, Shell's film projects weren't so different from the government's. One of its chiefs gave the rationale; Shell made films:

> because we believe in Australia and in Australia's destiny—
> because we think it is a good thing for the spotlight to be put
> on the spirit of initiative, adventure and comradeship displayed
> by these people in the outback in the face of great hardship
> and great odds. Above all, we make them because we recognise
> that Australia's future is Shell's future.[9]

The company produced a few films of explicit sponsorship, soft-sell advertising with the commercial purpose made open and obvious; there were, for example, two promotional items about Geelong, where a refinery was being built. However dated and polite these may look now, the local screenings in school and town meeting-places probably helped their communities towards greater confidence at the time. With its documentaries, the Unit was more ambitious. The first was made in 1949, a very curious essay called *Around a Gum Tree*. Laboriously, the narration (again from the quasi-English, teacherly male voice) connects the diversity of the country's occupations to that of the eucalypt—red river gum, snowgum, bluegum, stringybark, the trees of the deserts and plains. Actual people, miners, farmers and town folk are registered pictorially and briefly; they don't begin to become characters. The point is national promotion: Australia is presented as offering work, scope, possibility and prosperous futures. The second documentary was *The Back of Beyond*.

VI
EAST OF MARALINGA

The Shell company was highly conscious of publicity, and put energy into promoting *The Back of Beyond* while it was still in production; its making was a widely heralded adventure. In February 1952 the trade paper *Film Monthly* noted that Heyer was travelling with two camera crews and—extraordinarily—two poets to help him on the script, Douglas Stewart and Roland Robinson. Later that year the *Bulletin*, of which Stewart was the literary editor, ran a full page of the verse he had written along the Birdsville Track. Parts of that work survived into the spoken narration, which was largely written and edited by John and Janet Heyer.

Too little is generally known of Janet Heyer's contribution to the film, although John Heyer himself spoke of it extensively in interviews. She was effectively both co-producer and production manager—'spare technician, nurse and general handyman' her husband said—doing continuity and all other secretarial work, maintaining and working the crew's radio transmitter, and giving daily lessons to the children in the cast, who were locals recruited in Marree. (The Heyers' own children were left behind in Sydney with a nurse.) Not least, she was principal cook, with Henry as

Janet Heyer at the two-way radio: 'spare technician, nurse and general handyman'.

Out on the gibber plain, Janet prepares a meal for the crew.

her assistant; during the shoot, she got up at 5 a.m. daily to make breakfast for up to eleven people.

John Heyer repeatedly acknowledged her value as a critic, in the making both of the script and of the film at rough-cut stage. Ironically enough, it is because she was interviewed by *The Sydney Morning Herald*'s women's page (of 9 April 1952), as 'Mrs John Heyer of Beecroft', that we can get glimpses of life during the shoot. For her it meant four and a half months of sleeping in the open, learning how to make damper; living out of one small canvas bag, which also served as a pillow; two shirts (always called blouses then) and dungarees, one skirt for odd times in the townships when respectable dress was in order; hat and sunglasses—those, she said, were her 'beauty care', with calcium and vitamin tablets. In that interview, however, there was no reflection of her part in the production itself. In the period, her roles are worth remarking; this was that postwar time when men explored, played soldiers, built dams and office blocks, while women kept house, raised the kids and maintained family life as a matter of course. They, and not their men, were expected to provide security and forego adventure; but Tom Kruse said years later that it had been Janet, more than anyone else, who had held the production together from one day to the next.

The energy which is palpable in the outcome therefore owes something to her constant involvement. That energy has to do with the whole collaborative network: the relations of director with writers, with Ross Wood—a great cinematographer—and the composer Sydney John Kay. Heyer stressed in interviews that in his film making, the music was always integral, not something added in afterwards, and he said that he had communicated closely with Kay from the outset. Some have found the music track inappropriate, belonging to a suburban consciousness. The moments when it works best are those with Henry, the Aboriginal children and the gramophone; with Tom's dance; and the very different, darker moment with Malcolm and the remembered hymns in the ruins of the mission.

The film was launched nationally; Shell did much more than run screenings in Sydney. A new theatrette was opened in Brisbane, where *The Back of Beyond* ran for a year; town halls and school halls were hired; tickets were handed out at the company's petrol stations everywhere. In consequence, a production which was non-theatrical, in the sense that it had no presence on the commercial cinema circuits, was received and reviewed all over the country. The *Tumbarumba Times* commented that after taking in the film's account of the desert roads and tracks, the gibber plains and merciless heat, readers should understand that Tumbarumba 'wasn't such a bad place after all'. Guardians, Chronicles, Expresses, Heralds and Advertisers from Broken Hill to Innisfail, from Echuca to Northam, from Cairns to Kalgoorlie, all noted and commented on the screenings of *The Back of Beyond* in their school halls and local cinemas; they still had them then. From the commentary then, in the film's own day, it was clear that audiences reacted to the film's double aspect: the dimension figured by the desert in both visual and verbal poetry, the dimension of loss; and on the other side the balancing reassurance, centred on Tom Kruse, the women at the radio, their wholeness and ordinariness.

Through them, the outback was almost domesticated for audiences whose schooling had taken in the exploring sagas from the nineteenth century, and with them ideas of the desert as terrifying; 'the great Australian loneliness' in the words of the popular travel-writer Ernestine Hill. The 'vanishing race' was marginal; the major figures were pioneers and explorers. Everyone knew how the naturalist-explorer Ludwig Leichhardt had been lost forever, gone to an unknown grave; everyone knew the more terrible history of Burke and Wills, so tantalisingly close to survival when they met their deaths. In 1957 Patrick White's *Voss*—a stunning transformation of the Leichhardt mystery— intensified those stories, to the point where history and myth become entangled. In that framework, *The Back of Beyond* made the outback a more bearable presence; part of a known Australia for those who were never likely to go there, but who still wanted carry a sense of their own country as one stretching away beyond the suburbs into difficulty and adventure.

Grounded in its local meanings, the film moved off into the world, which was also the world of the Cold War. Public discourse was pervaded by the notion of the Communist menace. Behind the sunny, expansive landscapes being offered to postwar Australian society, there was the backdrop of political threat, intensified by the nightmare spectre of atomic warfare, the imagery of roiling mushroom clouds. And those were quite close; not long after *The Back of Beyond* came into circulation, the atomic tests began in the South Australian desert at Maralinga and Emu Field, sites far southwest of the Track, but still not too far outside the film's horizons. For that reason, too, its images of good humour and resourcefulness, the small triumph of Tom's arrival in Birdsville, made it even more welcome to its audiences in that time; a kind of normality was affirmed.

VII
THE LECTERN AND THE WATER-CART

John Heyer said in later years that the sequence he most prized in the whole film was that of the Kopperamanna ruins, and especially the image of the black iron frame of the lectern. The statement expressed the nature of his continuing, ruling ambition: he wanted to make cinematic art. The lectern image belongs with the desert iconography of Sidney Nolan, who had joined the Heyers on their first exploratory trip, and those desolations painted, with vivid compassion, by Russell Drysdale. It has nothing to do with the commission to capture 'the essence of Australianism' or 'the spirit of initiative, comradeship and adventure'. In ways he may not have understood at the time, Heyer had made a film that asked, and still asks, its audiences to remember hopelessness, to think of the Australian deserts as places we might visit and even live in, but still places in which some of us can never properly belong.

Thus *The Back of Beyond* both evaded and transcended its commission. The play of contradictions is dynamic: hauntings, deaths and disappearances, the practicalities of everyday life in the desert; the jazz from the gramophone; the high-flown narration, spoken from an urban position remote from that of Tom Kruse and his kind, and the palpable gap between them. For viewers in

Music while he works: Henry has the gramophone set up as he cooks.

the present, the historical discords are compelling: the social gulf between Tom Kruse and the implied world of the narrator; the seeming indifference of Tom and the station-owner to what we would see now as an inescapable back-story, the dispossession of the Aborigines, who seem in this tale to occupy such easy, accepted places. The film doesn't raise the question of how their way of belonging might be, or could have been different.

And there's the huge question which some did remember to ask: why, in the first place, attempt to found a community in this hostile environment? Attending to outback humanity, looking at ingenuity, persistence, good humour—the amiable, unpretentious qualities of colonial survival—the film nevertheless became an essay on imperialism's nemesis; a film about loss. After the critical triumph in Edinburgh, the reviewer for the *Birmingham Gazette* commented 'It is beyond my comprehension that people choose to live in this utter isolation.' But as Ross Gibson has written, all the main characters—black, white, Afghan and others—are seen to 'adapt to the dictates of the country'; they're not out to subdue it. There's an interesting kind of heresy in this. *The Back of Beyond* shows a fine indifference to Progress, the dominant secular doctrine of its day, and one of the insistent themes in those schoolroom documentaries.

Heyer was given a generous budget of twelve thousand pounds; enough to make his reconnoitring journey, research and write, assemble an excellent crew with the cinematographer Ross Wood, and put together powerful apparatus with a vehicle, a wind machine and portable film-tower. He could spin the storytelling over more than an hour; he could work outside the linear constraints of the familiar information film, use an unorthodox narrative structure, try for poetry and reach it. He and Janet travelled with Tom Kruse for three months before returning to Sydney to produce the shooting script; there was, Heyer said, 'a colossal problem of time'. In the small film world around them, there was gossip about Heyer's high-level preparations, and questions about the need for the elaborate production apparatus—heavy camera tracks, the portable tower for high-angle shots.

All those questions were answered in the outcome. The shoot itself involved a week with cameraman only, then five with the whole crew, working from base camps at Marree and Cooper Creek, and dealing with varying conditions of weather and terrain. Some shots involved laying planks so that, for example, the

The Leyland Badger.

camera could accomplish its purposeful track in to the dark fossil shell in the opening sequence.

It took a day to cover the 145 kilometres to Cooper Creek, another day the 22.5 kilometres further to Kopperamanna, where parts of the ruined buildings had to be dug out of the rising sand. At times they were fighting the sandstorms, and the camera-tower became twisted in the high winds. Sometimes a swirl of dust would cover the existing tracks; there were delays because of Tom Kruse's rather relaxed sense of time (he could be a full day late turning up, John Heyer said) and then once because the truck on the shore of the Cooper was found half-buried in sand, with its wheels and engine missing; the bits and pieces were found in a local fowlyard. The heat was often merciless, so that shooting was possible only in the late afternoons and early mornings. In the outcome, we could be looking at one of Tom Kruse's fortnightly journeys, or at two or more of the journeys edited together; this isn't clear.

In longterm consequence, there have been viewers who contend that *The Back of Beyond* is less documentary than a film-essay, in the same sense as the works of Robert Flaherty, involving re-enactment and elements of fiction. The comment responds to the film's wonderfully fractured nature. It is marked by odd dislocations, splits in the storytelling viewpoint, moments of strain and self-contradiction. The furrowed sand in the opening shots, and the elegant formal typeface form a signal at the outset; this is for a literate, art-film audience, and it is offered to tell that audience about an alien world. The narration is spoken by an actor, Kevin Brennan, using an upper-class British-Australian accent; and there's the strongly literary quality of the script.

In 1957, when Heyer was installed in London as an executive producer with Shell, he wrote an article called 'A Documentary Aesthetic.' It began:

> The image of Australia on the screen... is in essence the image of nine million people building a new nation on a continental land mass twenty-five times the size of Great Britain, levelled with age and isolated for centuries by oceans that roll in two thousand miles and more on every side... a young and vigorous people building on an old, isolated land.[10]

Heyer affirms that theme repeatedly. He dwells on the continent's inland geography 'from the burning glare of stony deserts to frozen gum-trees on snow-covered high plains...' and argues that Australian film making can offer something unique with such imagery as 'the twisted trunk of a struggling mulga tree, the dance and rush of a grass-filled whirlwind.' In this, however, he wasn't proposing a cinema centred on grand images of landscape; he was concerned with land and landscape as active elements in filmed stories. In his understanding, 'the essential Australia' was both the land—the inland, the outback—and the people who lived there. It didn't matter that they were a small minority of the Australian population; they were those who carried 'the spirit of initiative and adventure on which the young nation has thrived'. He deplored the tendency of Australia's publicists to focus on surfing youth and golden beaches; those, and the popular rural slapstick of the hayseeds tradition, tended to belie 'the true virility of the people', and 'the true image' of the country; that, he repeated, must be as it 'always has been, the image of Man against Nature.'

VIII
A FILM IN REAR VISION

Much has been written and said of the film since then. In 1987, when it was more than thirty years old, the academic journal *Continuum* published in its first issue a round-table discussion with four scholars, Ross Gibson, Albert Moran, Tom O'Regan and Brian Shoesmith. There's a certain charm about this event; they set off like four musketeers into an area of national cinema culture which remained a set of puzzles, something interestingly apart from the genteel costume dramas (*Picnic at Hanging Rock* and the rest) which had been claiming the centres of attention through the 1970s and early 1980s. I now reconvene that meeting, and take a place at their table, an invisible fifth.

Two of this group exercise immigrant perspectives: Albert Moran is Irish-born, while Brian Shoesmith came to Australia as a young English immigrant in the early 1960s. This may have intensified their curiosity and their responses; they are neither the first nor the last immigrant scholars to find more in Australian tales and images that the locally-born—too easily inured, afflicted by cultural-cringe—have tended to allow. At this time in the mid-1980s, Gibson is preparing an essay on the film, attracted by its orchestration of modes; he says it's modernist, primitivist, and surrealist all at once. Albert Moran is working, in both teaching and research, towards *Projecting Australia,* his book on government-sponsored documentary in the work of the DOI and the Commonwealth Film Unit. Tom O'Regan asks him how he saw *The Back of Beyond* in relation to the other films of the period, the late 1940s and '50s.

Moran responds that he finds the film 'such a rich variety', not easily comparable to the documentaries being made at the CFU. None of them, he says, were 'as rich or as interesting', and he recalled that while in the earlier postwar years 'Heyer and other documentary people at the Unit were making films that imagine the inland as the vibrant centre of Australia', a 'rich fertile centre' supporting other parts of the country and the world, this film presented a version of central Australia as 'desolation and infertility', a group of stories 'of things that haven't come off', typified by the lost children and the ruins of the mission. The major contrast is with *The Overlanders,* where the inland was a domain of promise.

Cast and crew at the Lutheran mission ruins.

There I'd interrupt: you need to think about what happened to the country after *The Overlanders,* to the changes in the way Australia was understood and seen from the late '40s on. The four agree that *The Back of Beyond* is more in tune with the 1940s than the '50s in style and in 'its community emphasis' (Tom O'Regan's phrase). Albert Moran thinks that the earlier decade was marked by 'a rich mixture of different modes' in documentary making, and he notes mildly that '*The Back of Beyond* is not homogeneous'. Later on in the fifties, he notes, work from the DOI and the Commonwealth Film Unit tended to employ unifying, voice-of-God narration, less interesting soundtracks.

Taking Moran's point about period styles, Ross Gibson complicates the suggested history. He argues that there was another, dissenting sensibility at work in the 1950s, something represented by *Voss* in fiction and by *The Back of Beyond* in film documentary: a kind of minimalist narrative, visible in some of the explorers' journals, a viewpoint centred on desert and desolation. Gibson is constructing a tradition; he sees the film in a line of descent from the writings of Sturt and Eyre, who stood outside the imperialist view of the wilderness as supposedly uninhabited territory, out there to be controlled and conquered. He contrasts the attitudes he finds in those explorers with the more orthodox position of Thomas Mitchell, intent on dominating the terrain, certain of destination and purpose. 'It's a surveying, road-building kind of progress. He wants to make sure his culture lays itself over that land permanently and dominantly.'

In Sturt's and Eyre's journals, and differently in *The Back of Beyond*, Gibson finds 'a much more humble narrative', and one that is the more forceful because it finishes only to start again: 'Every fortnight the story begins.' That's where he finds the film's singular value; it's not about heroic failure, and not about the conquering of territory, but about a matter-of-fact persistence with living in improbable, hostile conditions. The film's overall narration has to do with its imagery, and with the way Tom Kruse and others inhabit their settings; a certain openness, a sense of the provisional and possible. (I'd like to quibble about the humble part; given the middle class certainties implied in Kevin Brennan's narration, humble isn't quite the word.)

Gibson and Shoesmith both remember that in Britain, Shell's promotional strategies meant presenting the English countryside as a place for holiday motoring; the company associated itself with nature, conservation, the National Trust, the ethic of heritage. Clearly, they couldn't do that so simply in Australia, and not at all when it came to the outback; but they could present *The Back of Beyond* with confidence to a supposedly unified audience, people for whom Tom Kruse and his kind were knowable, parts of the world beyond the suburbs.

The four discuss the influence of Lorentz, and Heyer's way of taking up rhyme and rhythm in narration, the chanting of place names, the way the stories of the road crisscross the journey, meshing with the delivery of messages. Thinking of the lost children, Albert Moran asks 'how does this fit in with the narrative of the film?' and answers himself; the journey, he says, gives rise to its own need for storytelling, and then the stories 'crisscross the emptiness'. The others

Crew preparing the lost children sequence in the sandhills. Left to right: Warren Mearns, the unit electrician; Heyer and Ross Wood.

weave around, trying to find connections with the imagery of children lost in the bush in the Heidelberg school paintings of the late nineteenth century. Tom O'Regan insists on the differences; accurately, he relates the canonical Frederick McCubbin painting, 'Girl lost in the bush' to the ethos and politics of development in the place and time. The bush depicted there was in the hinterland of settlement. By contrast, the paintings that might be linked to *The Back of Beyond* are those that Sidney Nolan developed from the trip he made with John Heyer: the stretches of desolation, backgrounds to the Ned Kelly story; and Drysdale's version of the drover's wife, the lone female figure and the outback shanty.

Ross Gibson perceives differently; he sees a link with Sturt's perception of Central Australia as 'a kind of void area' where ordinary certainties break down; he invokes Patrick White's *Voss*, and the explorer's inscrutable final disappearance. 'Into the ocean of sand they went...' The desert is another world; and as the film shows us at the end with the Aboriginal teacher, it calls for another kind of knowledge. He finds its strength in the interrelationships between people and land, the way the arid outback is made 'neither ineffable nor alienating'. He also sees a link with the Azaria Chamberlain story, the baby taken by a dingo at the camping-ground near Uluru in 1980; their discussion is taking place only six years after those events. Remembering the fierce arguments round the headlines, I think it's a bit too easy to make that connection; but it occurs to me that if those punitive tribunals had taken note of the dingoes seen in John Heyer's night-vision passages, and spoken of at the Oldfields' station ('the dingoes are the biggest problem') they might have paused longer before finding against Azaria's mother. Those animals are impressive.

Malcolm Arkaringa wanders the ruins of the Lutheran mission, with memories of his childhood and Father Vogelsang's teaching.

The scholars contemplate Malcolm's lament in the ruins of the church, his elegy for Father Vogelsang, and the nature of the Aboriginal presence in the film. Ross Gibson comments on Heyer's readiness to deal with 'the complexities of voluntary integration and involuntary assimilation as well'. This, he says, was unusual at any time, but surprisingly so for the 1950s 'when Aborigines did not even have the right to vote'. That right, as well as other elements of citizenly status, had in fact been acknowledged variably across the polity since late colonial times; but the essential point in the comment holds. In 1954, the mid-century's defining moments in race relations—the breakthrough Freedom Rides of 1965, the vote on Aboriginal constitutional status in 1967—had still to come; multiculturalism had not been voiced, and despite postwar European immigration it was barely imagined. The 'vanishing race' was almost a civic doctrine; and it's not clear that anyone noticed, at the time, how persistently the film's details contradict it.

The astonishing fact yielded in the details of *The Back of Beyond* is that in the strung-out community of the Track, Aboriginal people—as fellow travellers along the way, as workers sharing tasks, shouldering loads and sharing a camping-place, cooking and eating together—are simply *there*, part of the world as of right. This is not the picture of race relations many of us experienced in the 1950s, and it's not the image of the period as it has been handed on to younger generations: staid, misogynist, racist, conformist. It's as though John Heyer, with a consciousness formed by his own ranging experience, could move and work in fine disregard of that climate.

Janet preparing a meal in a Bedurie oven—an iron pot set in the ground and covered with hot ashes.

Along the way, particular Aboriginal personages—Mary, the women in the camel-driven cart, Paddy and Malcolm—come and go; Henry, however, is there for the whole distance, and he has his own interests as guardian of the gramophone, a role maintained from the beginning of the journey to the end. He's made friends with that musical technology; he's a modern Aborigine. And yet, with that said, the film still carries the unspoken history like an undertow: Henry, Malcolm, Mary and their kind are among the dispossessed. The ruling policy of the day is called assimilation, which, in its avowed benign aspect, means the admission of the first Australians to the white man's idea of wellbeing; its undeclared meanings have to do with the imagined disappearance of Aboriginal culture and traditions. When Henry sits in the circle with the children, all clapping to Western dance music, you could see it as a moment in the story of their defeat. You could also see it as a part of long-negotiated Aboriginal survival, on terms which white society, with the best-laid plans, cannot entirely foresee or control.

The four scholars move on to discuss the representation of women in the film. They're rather endearingly determined on political correctness; in the 1980s academia they all inhabited, it was necessarily part of the climate. They take into account the established feminist criticisms of the bushman-centred stories and legends, in which men held the centre. Ross Gibson says:

> Unless I am misreading it women seem to be quite ancillary
> to the true narrative. It is obviously a problem. When you try
> to think of the modes in which the women operate in the film
> they're either exclusively domestic or innocent. The girls, also,
> are portrayed simply as innocents who should have known
> better, who should have been better acculturated. And the rest
> of the women in the film are domestic ancillaries.

Citing Miriam Dixson's feminist classic, *The Real Matilda*, Gibson suggests that *The Back of Beyond*, like the old standard histories of settlement, underrates the roles of women. He is mapping the feminist historian's critique over the film and its 'true narrative', as though the film was concerned only with the drive. But looking at Mrs Oldfield's operation of the radio, and that by the Birdsville nurse at the end, it couldn't be said that the women's roles as they are shown here are 'either exclusively domestic or innocent.' The woman in the Mulka store, briefly as we see

Prime Minister Robert Menzies (centre) and Shell Australia CEO, JRC Taylor, congratulate John Heyer (left) on the Venice film festival, *Grand Prix Assoluto*.

her, is hardly an ancillary; others are carrying young children as they move round the tiny communities, and therefore doing crucial work, life-maintenance. Even the ailing Mrs Mac, whom we hear but don't see, is still resourceful; she could operate the radio when she needed help, and organise a signal for the flying doctor. The world of the Track is a woman's world too, in that day when roles and styles were divided along gender lines far more sharply than now. Some viewers of today, coming to the film for the first time, say that the women of the Track are among its liveliest elements.

The discussion ends with the scholars contemplating the formal qualities of *The Back of Beyond*, particularly its ways of transmitting 'a powerful sense of offscreen space', so that what is seen 'is just one spot on a continuum...[Heyer] really was a sophisticated director.' It was that very sophistication that saved Heyer, and the film, from the prevailing Cold War pressures and paranoias; *The Back of Beyond* is a model of the liberal humanism which overflowed the political divisions. Menzies himself—no friend of the campaign for a revived local film industry—still attended the Sydney presentation of the Venice award to John Heyer.

In a later issue of *Continuum*, Stuart Cunningham praised Heyer's lucidity, his attention to the unheroic ways in which outback people constantly found ways to adapt, with a kind of 'tentative defiance' and 'the modesty of scale that humanity assumes along the Track.' Given those, Cunningham argued, we're looking at a story of persistence, an alternative to the martyrdoms which figure in the traditions marked out by Henry Lawson's 'The Drover's Wife' and the grimmer stories of Barbara Baynton. Drawing on those discussions, Ross Gibson wrote extensively of the film in an essay called 'Yarning', which formed a chapter in his book *South of the West*. Gibson called the film 'mythopoeic', and reflected that 'Heyer's version of the polyglot Outback is a description of a society which survives on its storytelling... a society with enough humility to acknowledge that the world of meaning and of responsibility to one's environment is larger than the capacity of any one person or information-storage system.'

IX
'POETRY AND EARTHINESS'

It should have been worth a modest headline—one small Australian film inspiring a whole book in London in 1968; but I don't think anyone noticed. Fourteen years after the film's emergence, the British Film Institute published a study guide to *The Back of Beyond*, written by Eric Else. This was evidence of a climate in which the purposeful, concentrated commitment to serious film study was possible; it could not have been done in Australia at that time. Else examines the film in twelve segments, using Heyer's shooting script; he draws on a long interview with Heyer by Alex Richardson, and thus gives the film back in the context of the tough conditions of the shoot: Heyer told there of the heat, the wind storms, the indispensable Tom's exasperating ways with time and schedules. Looking back on all of it, remembering the sequence at Kopperamanna, he said he'd achieved there 'the ideal cinematic fusion of poetry and earthiness'. All films, he said, should have that balance. The statements show how seriously he took the lines of inheritance running from Eisenstein through Grierson and Jennings. Perhaps they also express his consciousness that, with all that concern for 'a young and vigorous nation' and 'the true virility of the people' he had still made a film about loss.

Eric Else, from the distance of the late 1960s, noticed other things. As he saw it, the position of the Aboriginal workers—typified in the sequence with Henry, the gramophone and the children—should be discomforting for white liberal viewers, while 'the patience and passivity of the partially assimilated Aborigine' should evoke 'sympathy for his plight.' He noticed the way Heyer negotiated dramatic balance: after the sequence on the lost children, the film comes to the places where the mother and daughter, together, wait for the truck; and where the Aboriginal woman teaches other children, both black and white, about survival. As he read the film, questions of race relations were alive at its centre.[11]

Having settled in London as head of the Shell Film Unit, Heyer returned to Australia frequently, and in 1957 made *The Forerunner*, again for Shell, on the Snowy River irrigation scheme. This won him further awards at Cannes, Venice, and Turin, with a silver award from the newly-formed Australian Film Institute in 1958. This film, too, was strongly pictorial, with a visual echo of Soviet-era propaganda in massive images of dam-building. The title indicated a thesis, that the Snowy scheme was an important first step in dealing with the continent's extremes; and the opening montage included beautifully devised vignettes of unnamed citizens battling through the wreckage after floods, or facing up to defeat when the drought-stricken farm had to be abandoned. Some shots deliver eloquent mini-dramas: the farming couple standing looking at each other for a half-moment before climbing into the cart, the nameless woman clad as though for town in coat, hat and handbag; the outfit is part of the language of pathos. In the montage on the aftermath of flood, another woman is seen going anxiously through the contents of a drawer in a heap of broken furniture, the shambles of a house; then, with clear relief, she locates a ring and puts it on her finger.

We don't meet either of those women again in the course of the film. They are present not as individuals but in their roles, their typicality. *The Forerunner* is an instructional film of considerable eloquence—despite two rather stiff and sober segments in which a professor, with blackboard and pointer, explains the major irrigation scheme. There is, however, no commentary to overload the imagery; for that reason *The Forerunner* could have been an even better film than *The Back of Beyond*. But while there's no overriding narration, there's no Tom Kruse equivalent either, no human figure to travel with us through the sequence; we have a remarkable descriptive essay, but we don't have a story.

Heyer made plans for other films which would take up major questions for Australia: a version of Eleanor Dark's *The Timeless Land*; a film from Xavier Herbert's *Capricornia*; and a feature-documentary focussed on the situation of Aborigines. Perhaps race relations had by then moved from the margins to the foreground in the way he saw his country. The plans for *Capricornia* went a fair distance; Heyer's papers contain a long correspondence with Anthony Buckley, as prospective producer, and Heyer had chosen Stephen Wallace to direct. That *Capricornia* was never made can be justly lamented; it could have been a very good film indeed. Neither that film nor the others eventuated, though Heyer did make a long documentary on the Barrier Reef (*The Reef*, 1979). One question can be asked: how far were his larger ambitions broken and curtailed by the loss of Janet? She died of cancer in February 1969, at the age of fifty two; the notice in *The Times* of February 22 read 'after a long illness borne with outstanding courage.' They were a team.

There were other losses. *The Back of Beyond* owes its enduring cinematic eloquence, its stunning visual clarity, to Ross Wood, who worked on camera on several other films in the period, but was principal cinematographer on only two others, Cecil Holmes' features *Captain Thunderbolt* and *Three in One*. The first of those is largely missing from the archives, and is being sought; both were made under the near-impossible conditions of the later 1950s, when distribution and exhibition pathways were effectively closed to local production by the Hollywood-dominated block-booking system. Wood could have done a great deal more. Holmes' aspirations too were largely thwarted; Heyer, working in his own ways, got somewhat further. Hoping always for more, he made several good documentaries, and one great one. For that he was indebted, indispensably, to Janet Heyer, Ross Wood and Tom Kruse.

Janet intent on communication.

X

HISTORY LESSONS, SCENIC FLIGHTS

In 2004, marking the film's 50th anniversary, the National Film and Sound Archive issued a new DVD, adding in for good measure the seven minutes of *Journey of a Nation*; and *The Back of Beyond* found new audiences, sparking memories, stirring old history lessons. Tom Kruse had driven the Track in the same truck until 1957, when it broke down on Pandie Pandie station, just south of the Queensland border. It stayed there, stuck in place, until 1983; then a devoted group, Tom among them, determined to restore it, began a long labour of love. In 1986, at South Australia's 150th anniversary, Tom travelled the Track again, leading a convoy of 150 vehicles; he drove it once more in 1998—if not in that same truck, it was in another one like it, impressively painted green. Another film, Roger Clarke's *Last Mail from Birdsville* (2000), recorded the event. A legend in his lifetime, they said. Carrying the legend cheerfully to the end, Tom Kruse died on 30 July 2011; he was ninety six.

The Badger stood for a time by the old railway platform in Marree; it is now in the motor museum at Birdwood in Adelaide. The line to Marree went out of service in 1980, when the main central Australian railway was established 200 kilometres to the west; the town was much diminished. At the last count it had a population of seventy; but its position at the junction of the Oodnadatta and Birdsville Tracks guarantees a flow of tourism. Old rail carriages have been put to use as dwellings; there is a museum, a caravan park, and a replica of the first mosque, built from bush materials by the Afghans. Birdsville, population two hundred and eighty-three at the last count, has fared somewhat better; since 1970, the mail has come in by plane, and the scenic flights over Lake Eyre land there. Every spring, when thousands arrive for the Birdsville races, the town explodes with life, and the 1,700-metre strip is crowded with light aircraft. The Track is

Henry in the Chevrolet Blitz when Cooper Creek was in flood.

graded, but not sealed, and the massive 4WDs often arrive with punctures to be mended.

In the town's information centre, the film is screened regularly; and down the Track at Mungerannie, in October 2012, a tourist buying postcards in the pub noticed vivid, familiar images of sandhills playing on the TV screen in the bar.[12] A few locals were standing round, casually watching *The Back of Beyond*.

ENDNOTES

Fortunately, John Heyer (1916–2001) was an assiduous keeper of his own records and memorabilia. The National Film and Sound Archive (NFSA) holds twenty large boxes of these materials; these constitute a principal source of information for this essay, particularly including press responses to *The Back of Beyond* and Heyer's own career. The collection includes correspondence on films made and unmade, and records of Heyer's work in its different phases, successively with the Australian National Film Board, with the Shell Film Unit, and then with the London-based John Heyer Film Company. It is accessible at the NFSA at Heyer, John: documentation 246485.

1. There are many books on the work and influence of Grierson, beginning with Forsyth Hardy's classic *Grierson on Documentary* (1947). See especially Part 2 of *Imagining Reality: The Faber Book of Documentary*. *The Granton Fishing Trawler* can be seen at http://www.youtube.com/watch?v=LgNyUXSoCpY.

    After uncredited production work on *Housing Problems* (Edgar Anstey and Arthur Elton, 1935) Ruby Grierson (1904–1940) directed short documentaries for government agencies, and then for the war effort on the home front; she was known for her humorous and humane perspectives and for her ability to put interviewees, working-class women especially, at ease before the camera. At work on a film about child evacuees to Canada, she was killed when the trans-Atlantic ship on which she was travelling was torpedoed.

    Marion Grierson (1907–1998) learned film editing techniques from her brother while he was making *Drifters*, and then joined him at the Empire Marketing Board film unit; she directed several witty and elegant short films promoting tourism in Britain. In 1936 she became editor of *World Film News*, a short-lived journal that served the documentary movement and the beginnings of television.

2. John Heyer's early schooling in film history, criticism and theory is instructive for the present, when film production training is often believed to need to exclude those dimensions, to be strictly practical and technical.

    Heyer shared film society life and intensive reading on cinema with his close friend Damien Parer (1912–1944), who was more than an exceptionally gifted cinematographer; he had a strong sense of narrative and human character. His wartime films from the Middle East and Pacific battlefronts are enduring classics. Like Heyer, he was very interested in theoretical approaches to film and particularly in the ideas of Grierson. His best-known work survives in the Oscar-winning newsreel *Kokoda Front Line* (1943). He was killed in Palau in September 1944.

3. Dulkaninna Station, 84 kilometres north-east of Marree, covers 2,000 square kilometres; it has a long history in environmentally adaptive practices in cattle raising and management, and is also a centre for tourism.

4. The Royal Flying Doctor Service began in 1928 as the Australian Inland Mission's Aerial Medical Service, principally on the instigation of the Presbyterian missionary John Flynn. By 2012 it was operating 61 aircraft, employing a staff of more than 1,000, and flying almost 27,000,000 kilometres annually.

5. 'Father' Hermann Heinrich Vogelsang (1832–1913) was a lay missionary of the Lutheran faith; he ran an unofficial post office, conducted services for the Dieri (or Diyari), the local Aboriginal people, in their own language, and remained at the mission until his death.

6. Grierson's 'Memorandum to the Right Honourable, the Prime Minister' can be read in full in *An Australian Film Reader,* pp. 72–78; see also the interview that follows with Stanley Hawes, 'Grierson in Australia'. The Memorandum can also be read at http://www.latrobe.edu.au/screeningthepast/classics/cl0799/jg2cl7a.htm

Menzies' hostility to film probably had to do with the generally-held view that film work, particularly in documentary, was incurably biased toward the left.

7. For sharing her memories of the changing political climate and its effects on government filmmaking, I am particularly grateful to Roslyn Poignant. The effects of Cold War politics on Australian film production are discussed by David McKnight in his article 'Australian Film and the Cultural Cold War' in *Media International*, Issue 111, May 2004, pp. 118–130.

The best source for the history of government-funded documentary in the postwar period is Albert Moran's *Projecting Australia: Government film since 1945* (see bibliography).

The discussion surveyed here can be followed in *Continuum*, Vol. 1, Nos.1 and 3.

8. *The Valley is Ours* can be seen at http://www.abc.net.au/ aplacetothink/html/valley.htm

9. From the Shell website, http://www.shell.com.au/ our-history-in-australia: 'A question that teases many of today's employees is why did Shell ever sponsor or produce documentary films, especially about subjects that appear to be unrelated to commercial considerations? One answer was given by JRC Taylor, the head of Shell in Australia from 1955 to 1961, when looking back on such internationally acclaimed classics as *Alice through the Centre (1950)*, *In the Steps of the Explorer* series, *Rankin Springs is West* (1952) and *The Back of Beyond* (1954). "We make them because we believe in Australia and in Australia's destiny..." '

10. John Heyer's article 'A Documentary Aesthetic' appeared first in *The Geographical Magazine* for Spring 1957, and is reprinted in *An Australian Film Reader*. The Lutheran missionary presence in Central Australia, and the work of the missionary Carl Strehlow, are explored in Paul Carter's *The Lie of the Land* (Faber and Faber, 1996).

There are noticeable links between the film's imagery and representations of the desert in Sidney Nolan's photos, paintings and drawings, and in the paintings of Russell Drysdale.

11. Eric Else's point of view on the Aboriginal presences in the film is significant when we consider the changing perspectives at work in white Australia at the time. Dominant complacencies had been shaken by the 1965 Freedom Rides and the campaign around the 1967 referendum; but the view from a distance sharpens the poignancy of what Else terms 'the half-assimilated' position. In the film, it is there most vividly in the images of Henry with the gramophone; for him the 'music machine' is always the most important item in the freight on the truck.

12. For her recollection of the scene around the bar at Mungerannie, I am grateful to Anne Freadman.

BIBLIOGRAPHY

Cousins, Mark and Macdonald, Kevin, *Imagining Reality: The Faber Book of Documentary*. London: Faber and Faber, 1996

Else, Eric, *The Back of Beyond: a study guide*. London: Longman, 1968

Fitzsimons, Trish, Laughren, Pat and Williamson, Dugald, *Australian Documentary: History, Practices, Genres*. Melbourne: Cambridge University Press, 2011

Gibson, Ross, *South of the West: Postcolonialism and the Narrative Construction of Australia* Bloomington: Indiana University Press, 1992

Moran, Albert, *Projecting Australia: Government and film since 1945*. Sydney: Currency Press, 1991

Moran, Albert, and O'Regan, Tom (eds.), *An Australian Film Reader*. Sydney: Currency Press, 1985

O'Regan, Tom, *Australian National Cinema*. London: Routledge, 1996

Pike, Andrew, and Cooper, Ross, *Australian Film 1900–1977: A Guide to Feature Film Production*. Melbourne: Oxford University Press, 1998

Vaughan, Dai, *For Documentary: Twelve Essays*. Berkeley: University of California Press, 1999

White, Patrick, *Voss*. London: Eyre and Spottiswoode, 1957

Williams, Deane, *Australian Postwar Documentary Film: An Arc of Mirrors*. Bristol: Intellect Books, 2008

Continuum: a Journal of Media and Cultural Studies. Nos. 1 and 3, 1987, 1988

FILMOGRAPHY

Arrivée d'un train en gare à La Ciotat (A train arriving at the station at La Ciotat), Auguste and Louis Lumière, 1895

Coal Face, Alberto Cavalcanti, 1934

Drifters, John Grierson, 1930

Fires Were Started, Humphrey Jennings, 1943

The Forerunner, John Heyer, 1957

Forty Thousand Horsemen, Charles Chauvel, 1941

Germany Year Zero, Roberto Rossellini, 1948

Heritage, Charles Chauvel, 1935

Jour de Fête, Jacques Tati, 1949

Journey of a Nation, John Heyer, 1947

Last Mail from Birdsville, Roger Clarke, 2000

Listen to Britain, Humphrey Jennings, 1942

Moana, Robert Flaherty, 1926

Nanook of the North, Robert Flaherty, 1922

Night Mail, Harry Watt and Basil Wright, 1936

The Overlanders, Harry Watt, 1945

The Reef, John Heyer, 1977

The River, Pare Lorentz,1938

School in the Mailbox, Stanley Hawes, 1949

The Song of Ceylon, Basil Wright, 1934

Sous les toits de Paris (Under the roofs of Paris), René Clair, 1930

Thoroughbred, Ken G. Hall, 1936
The Valley is Ours, John Heyer, 1948
White Death, Edwin G. Bowen, 1936

CREDITS

Release year
1954
Production Company
The Shell Film Unit

Key crew

Producer, Director
John Heyer
Script
John Heyer, Douglas Stewart, Janet Heyer, Roland Robinson
Photography
Ross Wood
Music
Sydney John Kay
Production Assistant
Max Lemon
Assistant Director
George Hughes

Assistant Camera
Keith Loone
Sound
John Heath
Sound Supervision
Mervyn Murphy

Running time: 66 minutes

Key cast

(playing themselves)
Tom Kruse
William Henry Butler
Paddy
Bejah Dervish
The Oldfields of Etadinna
Malcolm Arkaringa
Jack the Dogger
Old Joe the Rainmaker
The People of the Birdsville Track

ACKNOWLEDGMENTS

I wish to thank Series Editor, Jane Mills, for her commission to write about *The Back of Beyond,* a highly rewarding task which has taken much longer than either of us imagined at the outset; it was interrupted by unforeseeable and uncontrollable circumstances. Through those, Jane has been magnificently tolerant and generous. I thank the staff of the National Film and Sound Archive for all their help and encouragement, with special thanks to Amanda McCormack. My thanks, too, to Senior Editor Paul O'Beirne at Currency Press for his professionalism and quick responses.

Thanks also to those who have shared and discussed this film with me: David Donaldson, Jim Masselos, Albert Moran, Tom O'Regan, Roslyn Poignant, Tom Waddell, Sarah Waddell, Stephen Wallace, Arief Utomo, Jeannine Jacobson, Julian Thomas and Sam Thomas. In London, my friends Tony Bremner and Peter Olney called in a digital-film genius to re-calibrate their viewer so that an Australian DVD could be played on it, overriding the regional barrier. At Pyndan Camel Tracks, outside Alice Springs, Julia Burke, Marcus Williams and their friends organised a screening under the stars, on a very cold Central Australian night; a somewhat crumpled sheet did duty as a screen, and we kept a fire going in the petrol-drum. And in Sydney the producer Martin Williams—the viewing companion of the opening paragraphs—went to some lengths to watch the film and discuss it with me; seriously ill with cancer, he took extra pain-killers and an additional stimulant to last him through the screening and afterwards. Many years of dialogue and friendship ended with his death, for me and others; now, in discussions around film and TV, we try to imagine what he would have said. One thing we know is that, as with *The Back of Beyond,* what always mattered most was the story.

Australian Screen Classics

'The Australian Screen Classics series is surely a must for any
Australian film buff's library'
Phillip King, Royal Holloway, University of London
Available from all good bookshops or from
www.currency.com.au

The Adventures of Priscilla, Queen of the Desert by Philip Brophy
ISBN 978 0 86819 821 7
In his provocative reading of Stephan Elliott's cult 1994 film, Philip
Brophy invites us to think more deeply about what this film is
saying about Australia, its history, its culture and its cinema.

Alvin Purple by Catharine Lumby
ISBN 978 0 86819 844 6
Australia's first R-rated feature film created a furore when it was
released in 1973. Catharine Lumby revisits claims that the movie is
an exercise in sexploitation and argues the films complexity.

The Barry McKenzie Movies by Tony Moore
ISBN 978 0 86819 748 7
An illuminating tribute to Bruce Beresford's subversive and
hilarious *The Adventures of Barry McKenzie*, and its riotous sequel, by
cultural historian and documentary-filmmaker, Tony Moore.

The Boys by Andrew Frost
ISBN 978 0 86819 862 0
Andrew Frost's monograph explores the achievements of this
award-winning film, placing its thematic concerns into a broader
context of social anxieties about violence, crime and morality.

The Chant of Jimmie Blacksmith by Henry Reynolds
ISBN 978 0 86819 824 8
Based on Thomas Keneally's award-winning novel, Fred Schepisi's
1978 film is a powerful and confronting story of a black man's
revenge against an injust and intolerant society.

The Devil's Playground by Christos Tsiolkas
ISBN 978 0 86819 671 8
Christos Tsiolkas invites you into Fred Schepisi's haunting film
about a thirteen-year-old boy struggling with life in a Catholic
seminary.

Jedda by Jane Mills
ISBN 978 0 86819 920 7
Many layers lie beneath *Jedda*'s surface and Jane Mills unpeels these, exploring the mysteries embedded in its story, soundtrack and images, making the film a classic of the Australian screen.

The Mad Max Movies by Adrian Martin
ISBN 978 0 86819 670 1
Adrian Martin offers a new appreciation of these classics: *'No other Australian films have influenced world cinema and popular culture as widely and lastingly as George Miller's* Mad Max *movies'*.

The Piano by Gail Jones
ISBN 978 0 86819 799 9
Writer Gail Jones' thoughtful and perceptive critique of Jane Campion's award-winning film, *The Piano*, assesses the film's controversial visions, poetic power and capacity to alienate.

Puberty Blues by Nell Schofield
ISBN 978 0 86819 749 4
'Fish-faced moll', 'rooting machine', 'melting our tits off': with its raw dialogue, Bruce Beresford's *Puberty Blues* has become a cult classic. Nell Schofield takes a look at this much-loved film.

Wake in Fright by Tina Kaufman
ISBN 978 0 86819 864 4
Tina Kaufman's essay explores how *Wake in Fright* was received on its first release in 1971. She also discusses the film's discovery after being lost for over a decade and its second release in 2009.

Walkabout by Louis Nowra
ISBN 978 0 86819 700 5
Louis Nowra says *Walkabout* 'destroyed the cliché of the Dead Heart and made us Australians see it from a unique perspective'.

Wolf Creek by Sonya Hartnett
ISBN 978 0 86819 9122
Sonya Hartnett weaves the fictional tale of *Wolf Creek* together with accounts of true murders and examines how the film is 'not simply a horror film, but a film in which horror happens.'